All rights reserved. Written permission must be obtained from the publisher before reproduction or transmission of any part of this book except for brief quotations in reviews, articles, or related publications.

Copyright 2003

Published by
Integritous Press
P.O. Box 5043
Phillipsburg, NJ
08865

Library of Congress Cataloging-in-Publication Data

Fantina, Steven P.
101 Words You'll Probably Never Need To Know But Can Use To Impress People/Steven Fantina, 1st ed.
ISBN 0-9745669-0-X
First Printing 2003

Printed in the United States of America

For all the Word of the Day (www.wordofthedaywebsite.com) subscribers who have allowed me to have so much fun and learn so much over the past five+ years, especially the many recipients serving in the United States military whose valiant sacrifices keep me and the rest of us safe and secure.

Acknowledgements

Special thanks to Joel Barbee whose inspiring talents prove that a picture can be worth far more than 1000 words even if the words are far from ordinary.

Thank you to Caitlin Selby for her invaluable proofreading assistance and to LaTonya Pegues and everyone at TCS Printing who helped this novice author navigate the publishing process labyrinth. Thanks also to all who helped in the composition, printing, or distribution of this work and to all who encouraged it to fruition when I viewed it as an elusive pipe dream. Despite the assistance of these efficient helpers, if any errors remain in the final version, they are solely my responsibility.

The Greek dramatist Euripides unambiguously declared "the language of truth is simple."

Herman Melville once scoffed "a man thinks that by mouthing hard words he understands hard things."

Winston Churchill believed "short words are the best, and old words when short are best of all."

And more recently prolific novelist Jan Karon, speaking through one of the characters in her *Mitford* series, admonished "keep it short and axe the big words."

But what do they know?

Ok, maybe that's a bit harsh in referring to some pretty bright bulbs, but the value of a large vocabulary cannot be overestimated. Maybe you won't have a need to use *rodomontade* or *quiddity* every single day of your life, but you never know when you'll encounter such a word. Reading through the classics or specialized publications yields abundant unfamiliar words even for the well educated.

Nobody likes a *philodox* who regularly peppers his or her dialogue with the likes of *louche*, *xian*, and *cicerone*, but a three-dollar word spent at just the right moment can purchase respect. (enough with the financial analogy!)

A *coxcomb* who regularly substitutes *osculate* for *kiss* or *hebdomadal* for *weekly,* is merely showing off. (And probably advertising his or her inferior knowledge more than anything else. Why else would one need to employ such *dithyrambic* word choices?)

However, there are times when a rarer-than-usual word is suitable and even enhances the idea being conveyed.

You can't tell the boss that he's a jerk, but refer to him under your breath as a *rantipole monad*, and even if he overhears you, he'll be stumped while you'll get the satisfaction of having delivered an intellectual putdown.

Unfortunately occasions that mandate an out-of-the-ordinary word generally come up unexpectedly, and the word must be readily available. Life does not pause for quick trips to the thesaurus. That is why it is important to constantly expand your vocabulary. After all no acquired knowledge ever proves useless. (High school geometry is the exception to the rule.)

The 101 Words contained in this lexicon are presented in a humorous manner that will hopefully facilitate their retention in your memory. No one can *vaticinate* when you'll ever be called upon to use *seraglio, lycanthropy,* or *porkpie*, but it pays to be ready.

If this collection meets its objective, you'll find it both an amusing diversion and a valued resource that you'll return to time and time again for simultaneous laughs and enlightenment.

A note on the pronunciation guidelines

We all may be reluctant to admit it, but trying to determine a word's precise pronunciation from a standard dictionary can be confusing. With umlauts, accents, dots, schwas, straight lines, foreign letters, and alien symbols--who hasn't been left wondering just how they got the "e" upside down anyway? Deciphering the correct way to enunciate a word from such a resource often relies heavily on guesswork.

For the 101 words included here, you won't have to spend all day pondering the pronunciations because no esoteric symbols are used. Each word is followed merely by an italicized phonetic spelling using the standard pronunciation of all letters. For example if you see a "B," it is safe to assume that it conveys the sound heard in "bag" rather than "subtle;" a "P" should elicit the sound uttered in "plant" not "pneumonia." Single vowels denote short pronunciation while duplicates or vowel clusters indicate long pronunciation. "E" should be pronounced like it is in "step." "EE" connotes the sound made in saying "jeep," and "OA" suggests the vocalization heard in "boat."

Finally, regarding the accent mark that we have always heard tells which part of the word to stress: do we really pick one section to articulate more forcefully in a two or three syllable word? Do we even highlight one word or syllable in a typical sentence? Is there truly a difference between **switch**board and switch**board**? And which one is correct? The pronunciation guides in this work forego such debatable regulations.

101 Words You'll Probably Never Need To Know But Can Use To Impress People

1) **MINATORY** (*min a tor ee*) -- menacing or threatening.

Those minatory clouds in the distance suggest that we are in for quite a storm tonight.

MINATORY

2) **ULLAGE** (*ul ij*) -- the amount missing from a container that would make it full.

Bartenders need to be alert for patrons who complain that the ullage is too large just to try and get a free refill.

ULLAGE

3) **PORKPIE** (*pork piy*) -- a brimmed round hat that is flat on top and usually made from felt.

The nerve of some people; that man actually tried to shoplift a leather wallet by hiding it under his porkpie.

PORKPIE

4) **FURPHY** (*fur fee*) -- a rumor or untrue report.

There is absolutely no truth to that ugly furphy about Pastor Greene and the church organist, but that hasn't stopped it from circulating widely.

FURPHY

5) **ORISON** (*or a zan*) -- a prayer.

An Orthodox rabbi opened the convention with an inspirational benediction, and a Baptist minister closed with an orison of thanksgiving.

ORISON

6) **BANDERSNATCH** (*ban der snach*) -- an imaginary, fierce wild animal or an uncouth and/or unconventional person--generally one who is viewed as a menace or a nuisance.

Dinner was going peacefully until we heard some bandersnatch belch all the way across the restaurant.

BANDERSNATCH

7) **MONAD** (*mon ad* or *mo nad*) -- a single unit or entity or a one-celled organism. **MONADIC**, **MONADICAL**, and **MONADAL** are all valid adjective forms.

I wouldn't recommend discussing complex subjects with Cousin Roberta whose brain is decidedly monadal.

MONAD

8) **PSITTACISM** (*sit a siz am*) -- mechanical, mindless, and/or repetitive speech.

After hearing so many accolades about the visiting professor, the class was expecting a rousing lecture, but his presentation was little more than stale psittacism.

PSITTACISM

9) **RUCK** (*ruk*) -- a jumble, indistinguishable gathering, the expected people, or followers of whatever is currently in vogue.

Our new bookkeeper is trying to piece together a valid accounting statement from the ruck of contradictory documents left behind by her clueless predecessor.

RUCK

10) **DIPTEROUS** (*dip ter es*) -- having two wings.

The people of Kitty Hawk must have thought that Orville and Wilbur Wright were out of their minds when they claimed that their **dipterous** contraption would actually become airborne.

DIPTEROUS

11) **CARYATID** (*kar ee at id*) -- a supporting column that is shaped like a female figure.

Some of the caryatids supporting the museum's patio were sculpted tributes to the heroic battlefield nurses who tended the wounded during the Civil War.

CARYATID

12) **TELAMON** (*tel a mon*) -- a supporting column that is shaped like a male figure.

The museum's telamons were divided evenly between Union and Confederate soldier figurines.

TELAMON

13) **PERUKE** (*pa rook*) -- a man's wig of the type worn in colonial days.

George Washington, John Adams, and Thomas Jefferson were great leaders, but could you imagine any modern day candidate wearing a peruke as he campaigned for the presidency?

PERUKE

14) **FLANEUR** (*fla nir*) -- one who loafs, dawdles, or is constantly idle.

Nobody was surprised when Georgia left her lazy husband, but why she put up with the perpetually unemployed flaneur for almost five years is anybody's guess.

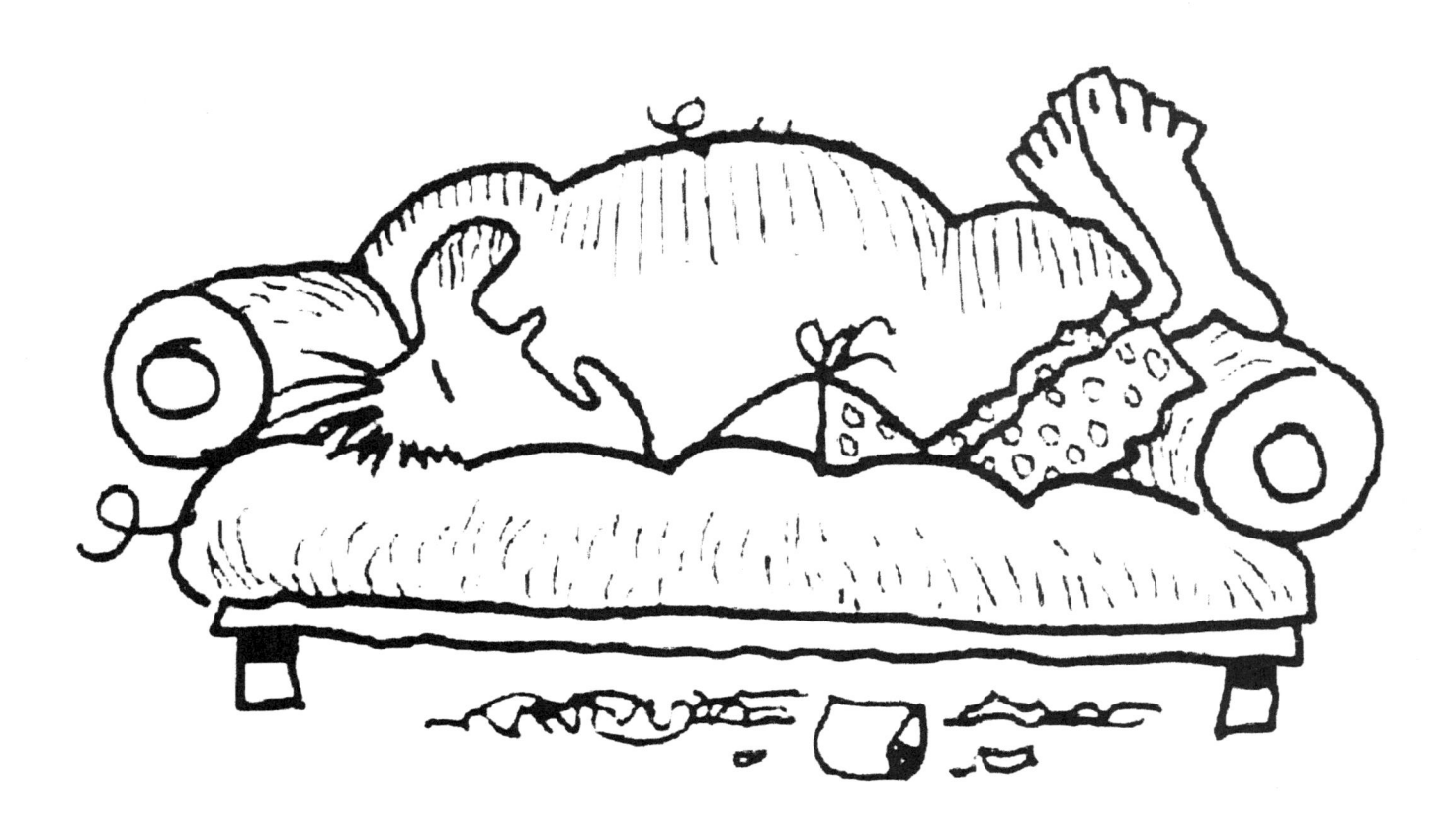

FLANEUR

15) **NUMINOUS** (*noo me nes*) -- divine, sacred, supernatural, or appealing to the highest human interests or pursuits.

The **numinous** call to serve in the military is answered by the nation's most heroic citizens.

NUMINOUS

16) **PROSCENIUM** (*pro see nee em*) -- the part of a stage in front of the curtain, the entire stage in ancient times, the arch or wall separating the stage from the audience, or foreground. **PROSCENIA** is the plural.

Jugglers performed on the proscenium to keep the audience from becoming restless while work crews changed the elaborate sets between acts.

PROSCENIUM

17) **APOTROPAIC** (*ap e tra pay ik*) -- designed to avert evil.

Stella's superstitions never bothered her coworkers until she became convinced that the mailroom clerk was a vampire and started wearing a garlic necklace for apotropaic purposes.

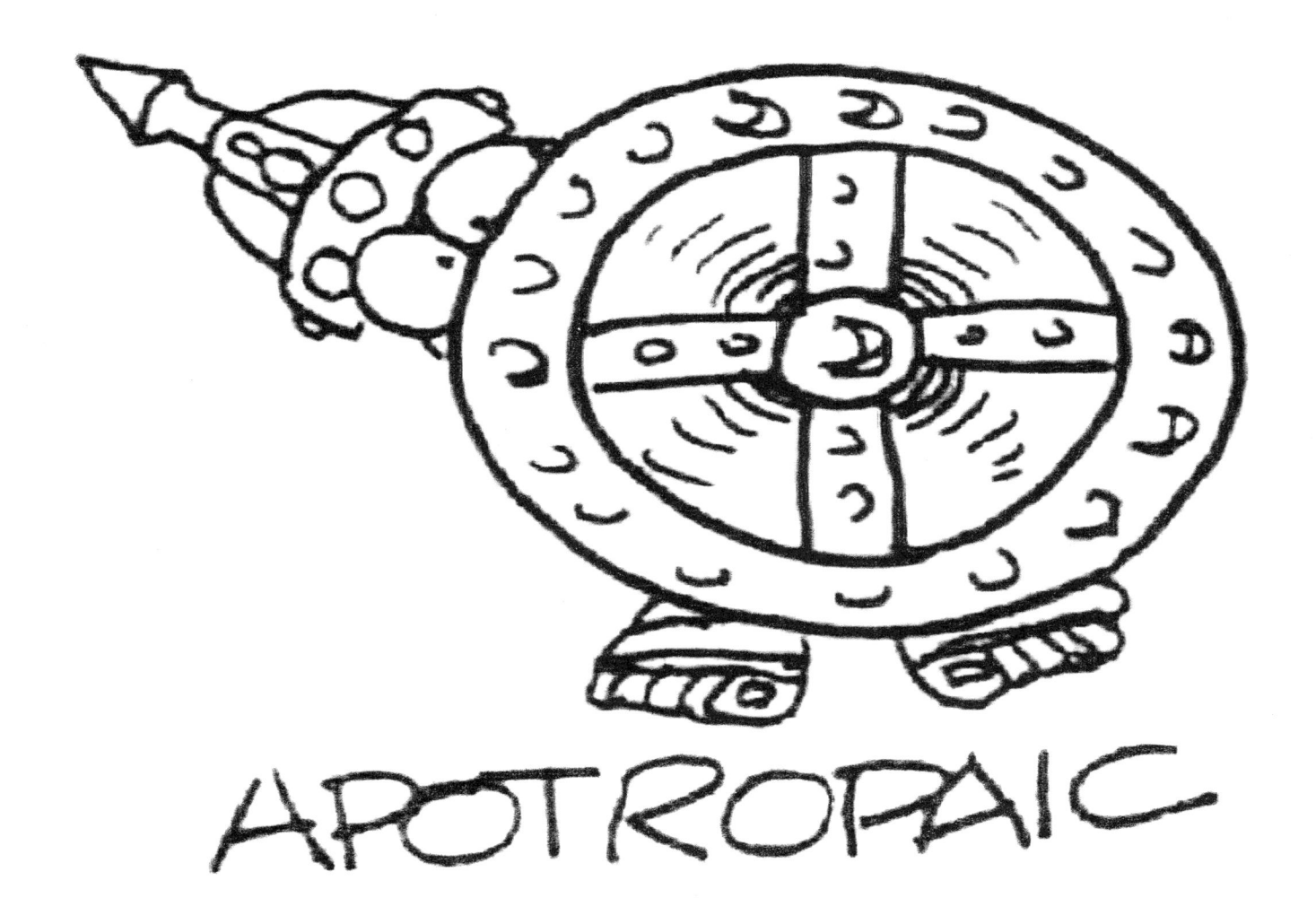

APOTROPAIC

18) **RODOMONTADE** (*rod a mon tayd*) -- blustering, bragging, ranting, or a boastful speech.

About twenty minutes into Alvin's repetitive **rodomontade**, it was obvious that no one at the cocktail party was paying attention, but the blowhard was undeterred and carried on with his tedious tale.

RODOMONTADE

19) **QUIDDITY** (*kwid it tee*) -- essence, eccentricity, or controversial minor point.

It was ridiculous the way Ryan and Carol argued over the title of Elvis Presley's last hit single, but **quiddities** have a way of getting under the skin.

QUIDDITY

20) **COXCOMB** (*koks koem*) -- a foolish or conceited person, or a jester's hat.

I can't believe that almost fifty people actually paid to hear some coxcomb give a talk allegedly proving that the world is flat, nor can I believe that an ivy league university sponsored the presentation.

COXCOMB

21) **PHAETON** (*fay i tn*) -- a light, 4-wheeled, horse-drawn carriage, or a vintage automobile.

There is something truly amazing about touring the Amish Country in the 21st century and seeing phaetons and cars traveling side by side.

PHAETON

22) **HEBDOMADAL** (*heb dom a dl*) -- weekly or a weekly periodical.

As difficult as it can be for Grandma to get out in the cold winter months, she never misses her hebdomadal journey to church on Sundays.

HEBDOMADAL

23) **GEWGAW** (*gyoo go*) -- a bauble, trinket, or something that is useless or gaudy.

Clara's attic must be cluttered with all the gewgaws she has brought back from her travels all over the world.

GEWGAW

24) **ECHOLALIA** (*ek oe lay lee a*) -- the compulsion to repeat immediately every word one hears or the process where a child learns to speak by repeating sounds. **ECHOLALIC** is the adjective.

Uncle Dexter has to keep his stevedore vocabulary in check whenever he visits the kids because the echolalic effects can be very embarrassing.

ECHOLALIA

25) **PIED-A-TERRE** (*pee a de ter*) -- temporary lodging or a secondary residence. **PIEDS-A-TERRE** is the plural.

Glenn and Monica eagerly looked forward to retiring early and opening a bed and breakfast, but they've found that running a pied-a-terre is more work than they ever imagined.

PIED-A-TERRE

26) **CYNOSURE** (*si na schoor*) -- the center of attention or something that guides or directs.

Beatrice hated being the cynosure, but when your pants fall down in the middle of a crowded grocery store people are going to notice.

CYNOSURE

27) **DADA** (*da da*) -- artwork or literature that is intentionally irrational or rejects traditional aesthetic values.

That so-called experimental artist became indignant when Howard said "it's called **dada** because anyone who can talk better than that could also paint a lot better."

DADA

28) **BILLET-DOUX** (*bil ee doo*) -- a love letter.

Somehow, a billet-doux sent via email never seems to make the same impact as a hand-written note.

BILLET-DOUX

29) **RANTIPOLE** (*ran ti poel*) -- a reckless or ill-behaved person, boisterous, excessively rude, or to act irresponsibly.

We had all repeatedly warned Harvey about his aggressive driving to no avail; hopefully losing his license for six months will change his rantipole ways.

RANTIPOLE

30) **ABSQUATULATE** (*ab skwoch a layt*) -- to depart hastily or abscond.

The police are looking for Dennis because he was asked to deposit the day's earnings but **absquatulated** with the money instead.

ABSQUATULATE

31) **CAUDA** (*kou da* or *ko da*) -- a tail or tail-like attachment.

Cauda seemed like a cute, if somewhat ironic, name for that tailless stray cat that moved into my garage.

CAUDA

32) **EPIPHENOMENON** (*ep a fa nom a non*) -- a secondary or additional symptom arising during the course of an illness or any secondary development. The plural can be either **EPIPHENOMENONS** or **EPIPHENOMENA**.

Eleanor's ever growing list of epiphenomena is either indicative of abundant complications or more likely further proof that she is an incurable hypochondriac.

EPIPHENOMENON

33) **FRUGIVOROUS** (*froo jiv er es*) -- fruit eating.

Some frugivorous creature climbed the orange tree and had a gluttonous feast last night.

FRUGIVOROUS

34) **JACTITATION** (*jak ti tay shen*) -- false boasting or an uncontrollable tossing of the body. **JACTATION** (*jak tay shen*) is a synonym.

Most of the family kept a straight face when Aunt Harriet explained that she was taking a belly dancing class to help lose weight, but the thought of a fifty-something, heavyset woman bedecked in a sari engaging in rampant jactitations did elicit a few chuckles from those lacking excessive willpower.

JACTITATION

35) **XIAN** (*shyan*) -- a beneficent spirit who travels the world performing good deeds based in the beliefs of ancient Chinese religions. It can also be spelled **HSIEN**.

Paul is convinced that a xian was in the car with him because he has no idea how he managed to swerve out of the tractor trailer's path.

XIAN

36) **OSCULATE** (*os kya layt*) -- to kiss or to come into close contact.

Mr. Smithers informed his secretary that she could hang mistletoe over her desk but "no osculating in the office."

OSCULATE

37) **LEXEME** (*lek seem*) -- a word, a linguistic base or unit, or an item in one's vocabulary.

When reading a book, you should look up every unfamiliar lexeme in a dictionary rather than just skip over it.

LEXEME

38) **GRISAILLE** (*gri ziy* or *gri zail*) -- a painting, stained glass window, photograph, or any artistic work done in only one color that uses shading techniques for emphasis.

You wouldn't think that a rainbow would lend itself to the grisaille form, but that picture hanging in the lobby is absolutely captivating.

GRISAILLE

39) **ULULATE** (*ul ye layt*) -- howl, wail, or intensely lament. **ULULANT** is the adjective form.

Beagle owners know that the breed ululates the loudest when the dog is happy.

ULULATE

40) **SERAGLIO** (*se ral yo*) -- a sultan's palace or a room or section in a household reserved for women--often a harem--in some Arabic countries.

Certain seraglios that were built over a thousand years ago are still functioning in their original capacity, and in a few cases the current inhabitants are direct descendents of the first occupants.

SERAGLIO

41) **OBJICIENT** (*ob jis ee ent*) -- one who objects or an opponent to a proposal or measure.

Objicients came out in full force to try and prevent the town council from widening Highway 44.

OBJICIENT

42) **ECLOGUE** (*ek log*) -- a pastoral-themed poem, often one in which shepherds speak to each other.

"Mary Had a Little Lamb" has to be the most famous eclogue ever written.

ECLOGUE

43) **PNEUMATOLOGY** (*noo ma tol a jee*) -- the study, theories, and/or doctrine of the spiritual world or theologically the study of the Holy Spirit.

Father Sebastian finds that sitting in a quiet natural setting with birds chirping in the background frees his mind of daily worries and greatly enhances his pneumatological reading.

PNEUMATOLOGY

44) **SIMULACRUM** (*sim yu lak rem*) -- a passing resemblance, trace, representation, or image.

Four people incorrectly identified Marcus as the bank robber, and even family members acknowledged a simulacrum between the two men.

SIMULACRUM

45) FLOCCINAUCINIHILIPILIFICATION
(*flok se no se ne hil e pil e fi kay shen*) -- the estimation of something as having no value.

The legacies of Sodom and Gomorrah stand as a warning of what can happen to a city when a collective floccinaucinihilipilification towards God's laws envelops its populace.

FLOCCINAUCINIHILIPILIFICATION

46) **PLONK** (*plongk*) -- cheap or low-quality wine.

Since the Jacobsens are not exactly wine connoisseurs, they would probably prefer some five-dollar plonk in a fancy decanter to an expensive bottle of dry chardonnay.

PLONK

47) **CAMARILLA** (*kam a ril a*) -- an unofficial group of advisers who are often clandestine and of questionable repute.

Not one member of the newly elected governor's influential camarilla has any government experience or even much of a grasp on current events.

CAMARILLA

48) **ZUGZWANG** (*tsook tsvang*) -- a situation in chess from which any move will cost the moving side a piece or maneuver it into an unwelcome position, or any situation in which it is impossible to take a step that has no detrimental value.

A philandering husband will quickly find himself trapped in a zugzwang from which there is no escape.

ZUGZWANG

49) **THEOMORPHIC** (*thie a mor fik*) -- having the appearance of a deity. **THEOMORPHISM** is the noun form.

Reportedly, Cecil B. DeMille agonized over the best way to reverently portray theomorphic scenes while filming his classic *The Ten Commandments*.

THEOMORPHIC

50) **QUANGO** (*kwang go*) -- a government agency or organization that operates autonomously.

Many Americans believe that the IRS needs to be completely overhauled because the **quango** seems to surpass itself in incompetence daily.

QUANGO

51) **BILLINGSGATE** (*bil ingz gayt*) -- abusive or vulgar language.

As one reviewer put it, "if you took out all the billingsgate, this 500-page novel would become a short story."

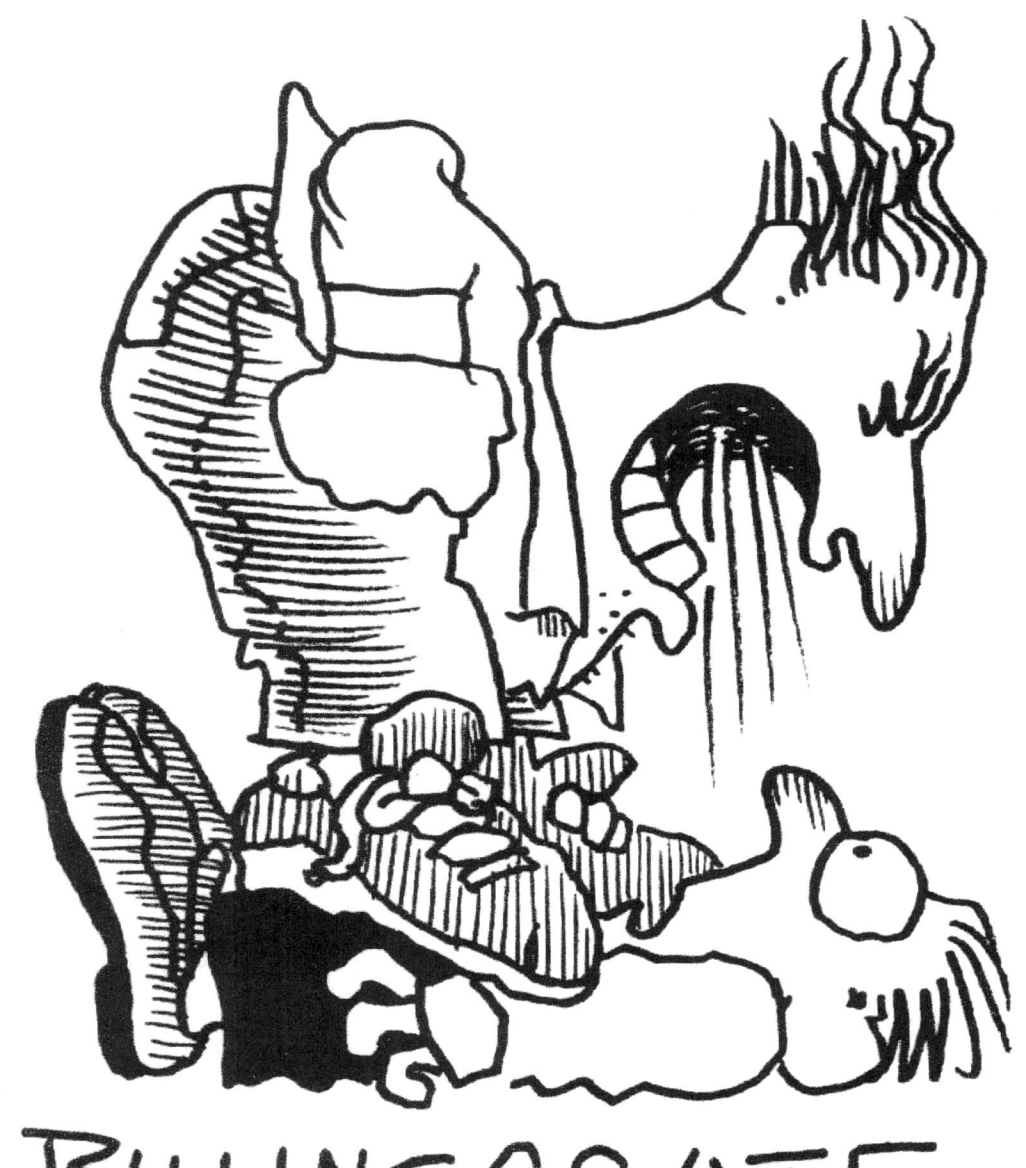

BILLINGSGATE

52) **PHILODOX** (*fil a doks*) -- a lover of fame, glory, or one's own opinions.

Any doubts that Maurice is a certified philodox vanished when we visited his house where his portrait hangs in every room, and a life-sized sculpture of his likeness overlooks the pool!

PHILODOX

53) **BRUXISM** (*bruk siz am*) -- involuntary grinding of one's teeth generally when stressed or sleeping.

Walter's bruxism was so loud last night that his wife eventually decided to sleep on the couch.

BRUXISM

54) **DEPILATE** (*dep a layt*) -- to remove hair.
DEPILATORY (*di pil a tor ee*) is the adjective form and also means an agent that removes hair.

Most men will discover that the aging process is a natural depilatory.

DEPILATE

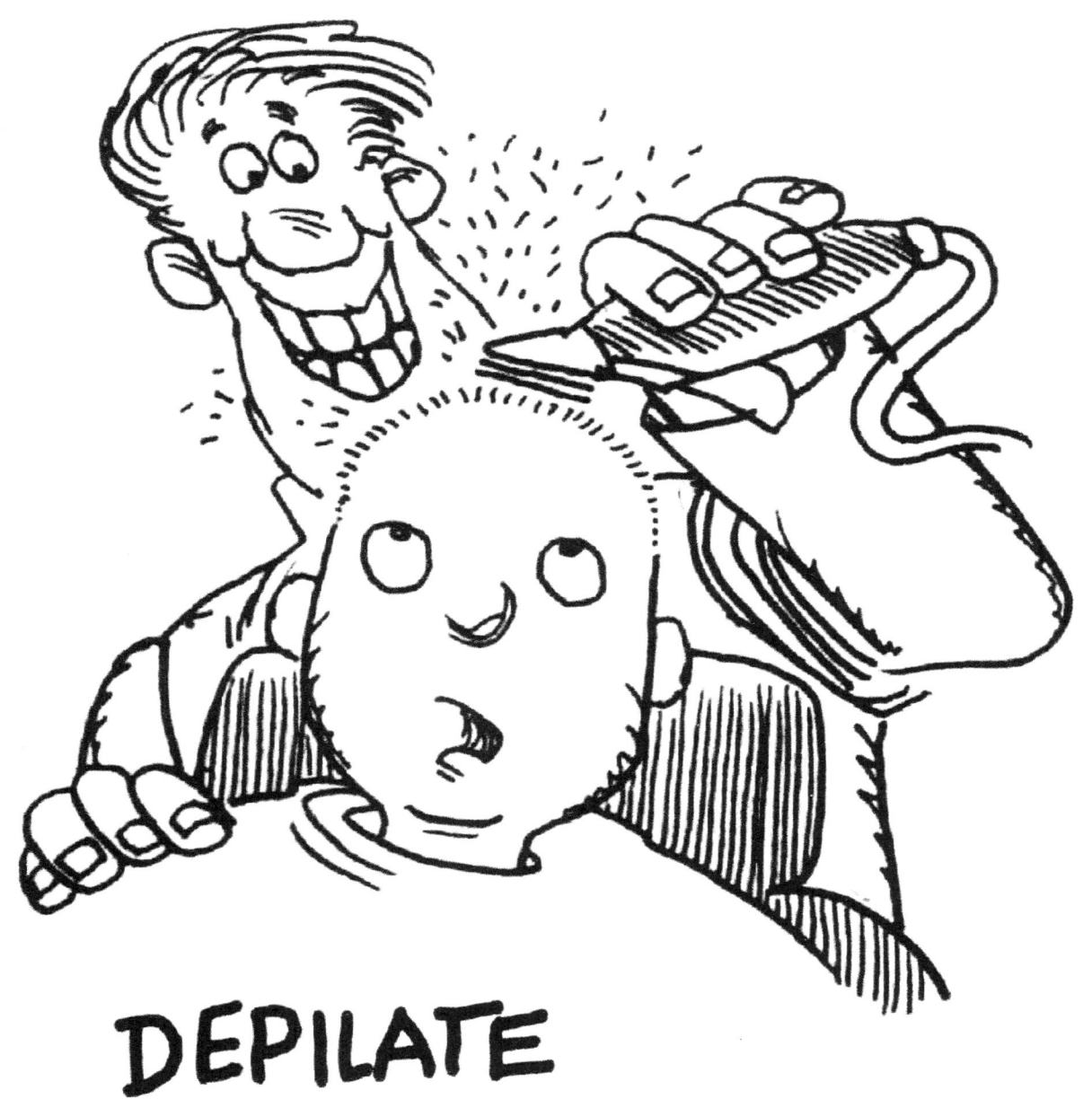

55) **ELEEMOSYNARY** (*el a mos a nar ee*) -- provided by charity, dependent upon charity, or relating to charity.

Few eleemosynary organizations even compare to the Salvation Army in terms of efficiency or thriftiness.

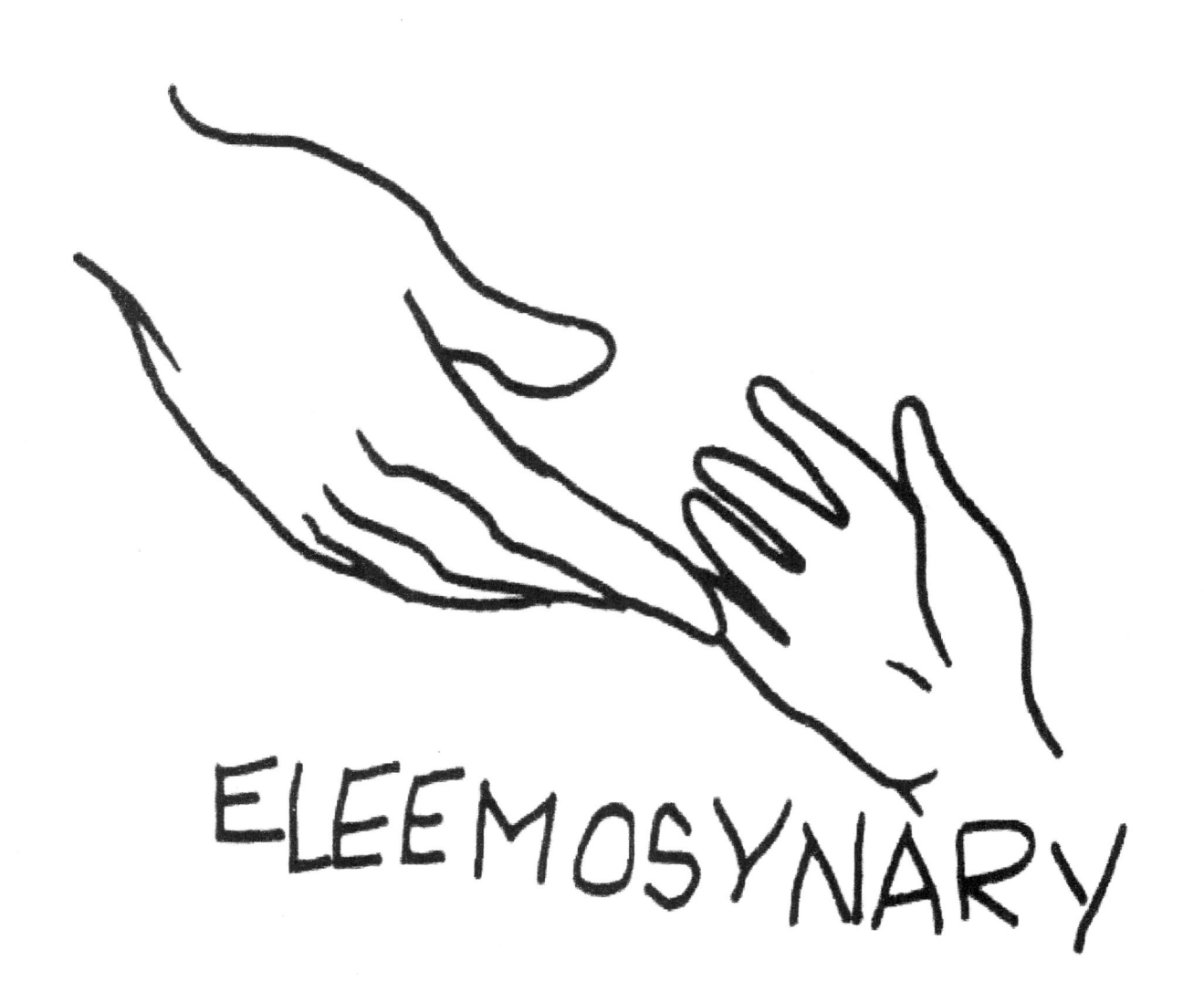

ELEEMOSYNARY

56) **DITHYRAMBIC** (*dith a ram bik*) -- wildly enthusiastic or irregular. The noun form **DITHYRAMB** also means a poem with an impassioned theme or abnormal form, or an ancient Greek song with similar characteristics.

Dithyrambic fans lined up at the airport in the wee hours to greet the winning team's plane when the players returned from their Super Bowl victory.

DITHYRAMBIC

57) **HEGIRA** (*hi jiy ra*) -- a trip to a more desirable location. It can also be spelled **HEJIRA**.

I can't recall anything that made me feel as patriotic as listening to those Cuban refugees describe their dangerous hegira on a makeshift raft and the new life that they've built here in America.

HEGIRA

58) **MISOLOGY** (*mi sol a jee*) -- hatred of enlightenment, reasoning, or persuasion.

How ironic that so many universities--institutions allegedly devoted to advanced scholarship--have become havens of misology where any views outside the politically correct orthodoxy are condemned as subversive and silenced.

MISOLOGY

59) **TERGIVERSATION** (*ter ji ver say shon*)
-- reversal of opinion, flip-flopping on an issue, evasive action or statement, or ambiguous answer.

Ernie had always opposed the death penalty but underwent a tergiversation after experiencing the callous indifference of some of those murderers he met while doing volunteer literacy training at the prison.

TERGIVERSATION

60) **IATROGENIC** (*iy a tra jen ik*) -- accidentally caused by medical treatment or resulting from the physician's diagnoses, manner, or actions.

Iatrogenic maladies can sometimes be far more serious than the initial source of discomfort.

IATROGENIC

61) **LIVERISH** (*liv er ish*) -- disagreeable, angered, or melancholy.

The stewardesses couldn't imagine why so many passengers were in such a liverish mood on this morning's flight, but there was simply no satisfying them.

LIVERISH

62) **MUSCIFORM** (*moo si form*) -- resembling a fly or resembling moss.

Alphonse isn't the most exciting person I have ever met, but saying he has a musciform personality is going a bit too far.

MUSCIFORM

63) **VENIRE** (*va niy ree*) -- a jury member, a person summoned to appear on a jury, or the list from which potential jurors are selected.

At first it looked like we'd have a hung jury, but the venires discussed the case in great detail and three days later announced their guilty verdict.

VENIRE

64) **LOUCHE** (*loosh*) -- disreputable, indecent, or shady.

Wouldn't it be refreshing to turn on a daytime talk show that celebrated the wholesome rather than exploited the louche?

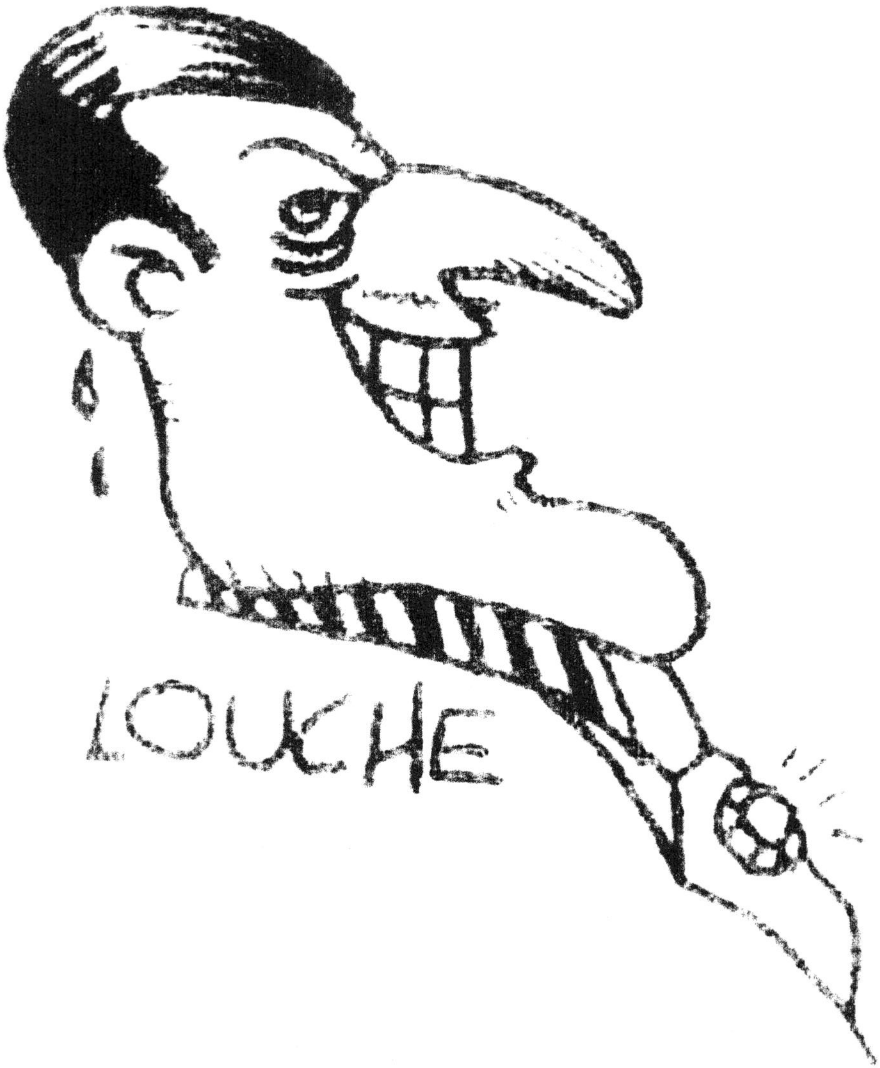
LOUCHE

65) **SAMIZDAT** (*sa miz dat*) -- an underground publishing system of forbidden material in the former Soviet Union, or any literature published without official sanction.

Official newspapers in the U.S.S.R. were little more than propaganda rags, but legions of brave, clandestine journalists kept the public informed through widespread samizdat periodicals that today provide an accurate, historic record of the Evil Empire.

SAMIZDAT

66) **CRYPTOZOOLOGY** (*krip to zo ol a jee*) -- the study or investigation of creatures whose existence is questionable such as Big Foot.

Cryptozoologists have long debated the authenticity of the Loch Ness Monster without reaching a consensus.

CRYPTOZOOLOGY

67) **STULTILOQUENCE** (*stul til ek wens*) -- foolish talk or babble.

Most political commercials are little more than extensively rehearsed, sophisticatedly packaged stultiloquence.

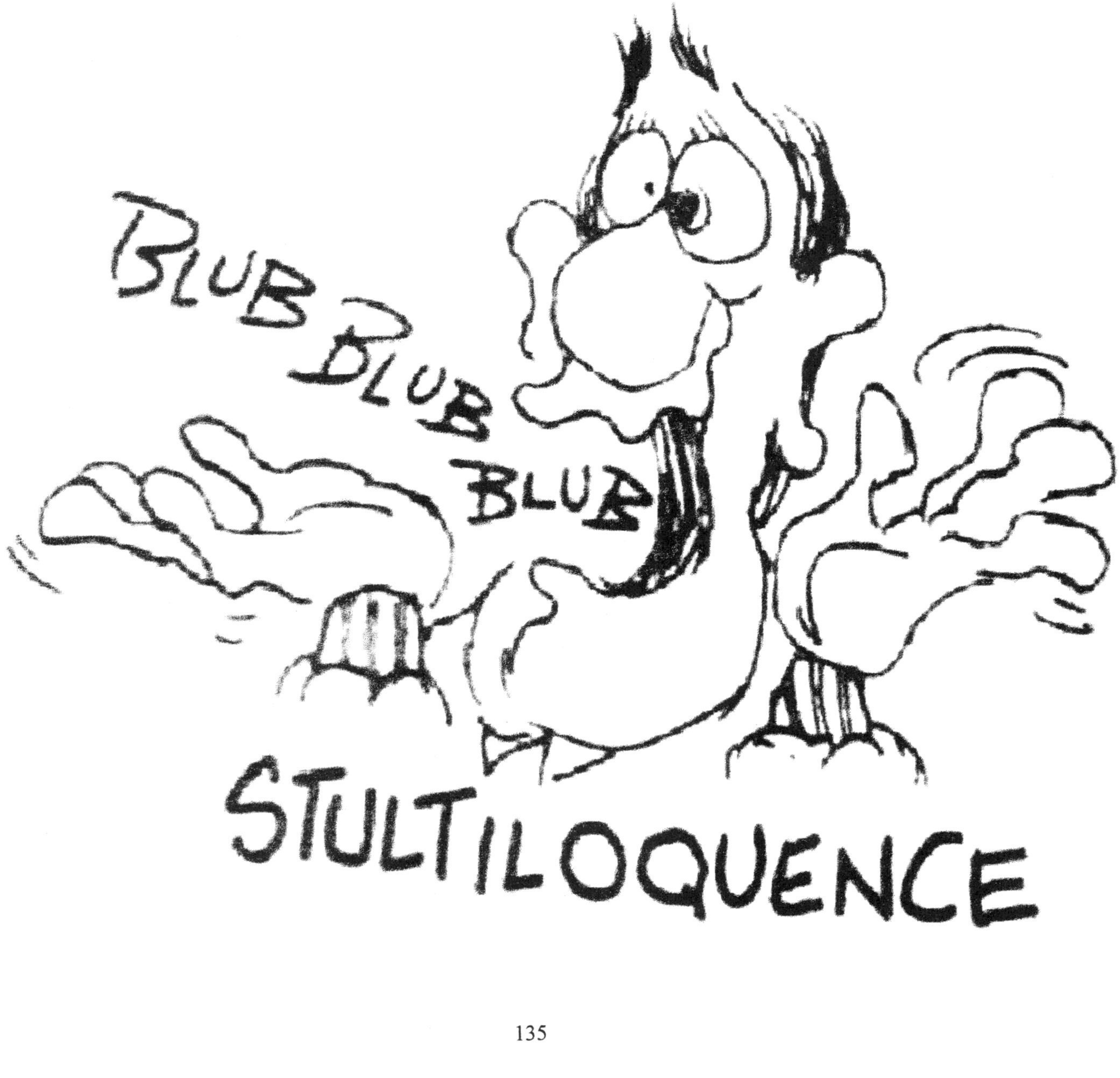
BLUB BLUB BLUB
STULTILOQUENCE

68) **ENTHEOS** (*en thee os*) -- inspiration or indwelling divine power.

Each of the Founding Fathers must have been guided by the same entheos as they collectively orchestrated the new government back in 1776.

ENTHEOS

69) **TRANTER** (*trant er*) -- a vendor who uses a horse-drawn cart.

The advent of the automobile was a major impediment to the tranter's trade.

TRANTER

70) TINTINNABULATION
(*tin ti nab ye lay shan*) -- the ringing of bells or a jingling sound reminiscent of a bell.

Hal was an avowed atheist who nonetheless always enjoyed the sound of Christmas Eve tintinnabulation emanating from all the church towers across the city, and one year the bells lured him inside where his resistance succumbed.

TINTINNABULATION

71) **CREPUSCULAR** (*kri pus kye ler*) -- indistinct, dim, or relating to twilight. **CREPUSCULE** as a noun means dusk or twilight.

Although Juan remembered meeting the suspect briefly, his recollection was crepuscular at best.

CREPUSCULAR

72) **SOUPCON** (*soop son*) -- a hint or trace generally of a flavor.

While the Chicken may have been marinated in Chablis, no one detected the slightest soupcon of wine.

SOUPCON

73) **ZYMOSIS** (*zy mo sis*) -- fermentation or a spreadable disease. **ZYMOTIC** is the adjective form.

St Elizabeth's School decided to close for a week in February after some zymosis had infected nearly half of the student body, and it seemed counterproductive to hold classes as scheduled.

ZYMOSIS

74) **SATURNALIA** (*sat ar nay lee a*) -- orgy or very wild celebration, or when capitalized it is the ancient Roman festival honoring Saturn the god of agriculture.

Frat parties too often descend into saturnalias where enough beer is consumed to empty the average brewery.

SATURNALIA

75) **PARADIDDLE** (*par a did l*) -- a drum exercise usually alternating left and right hand strokes.

Mrs. Hammerstein regretted renting her spare room to a drummer when he started practicing his paradiddles late at night.

PARADIDDLE

76) **ENOLOGY** (*ee nol a jee*) -- the science of wine and wine making. It can also be spelled **OENOLOGY**.

It is not just enologists, but specialists in a variety of medical sciences, who agree that the moderate consumption of wine provides numerous health benefits.

ENOLOGY

77) **GRIFFONAGE** (*grif on aj*) -- illegible handwriting.

Henry left us two pages of written directions, but we could not decipher his griffonage and never made it to the meeting.

GRIFFONAGE

78) **JEHU** (*jee hyoo*) -- the driver of a taxi or a coach, or any fast driver.

Yvette gave the jehu a fifty dollar reward because the good samaritan noticed that she had left her purse on the seat and drove back to try and find her.

JEHU

79) **LYCANTHROPY** (*liy kan thra pee*) -- the belief that one is a wolf.

Romulus and Remus understandably grew up with a severe case of lycanthropy.

LYCANTHROPY

80) **TAXONOMY** (*tak son a mee*) -- the science of classification, or the act of classifying things (generally animals or plants) based upon natural relationships.

The platypus presented a challenge to taxonomists because it is one of the very few mammals that reproduces by laying eggs.

TAXONOMY

81) **AQUILINE** (*ak wa liyn*) -- eagle-related, resembling an eagle, or specifically shaped liked an eagle's beak.

Benjamin Franklin's suggestion that the turkey be adopted as the national symbol was wisely rejected, and the bald eagle was selected, giving America a much more appropriate aquiline image.

AQUILINE

82) **JEFE** (*hay fay*) -- leader, boss, or chief.

Many workers resented paying their union dues because they believed their jefe was misappropriating them to support his luxurious travels.

JEFE

83) **TIFFIN** (*tif in*) -- lunch, or to eat, serve, or provide lunch.

The Parkers said that their most memorable Thanksgiving ever was the year they spent tiffining the homeless at a local soup kitchen.

TIFFIN

84) **PARAPH** (*par af*) -- a distinctive flourish or squiggle that follows a signature--originally used to reduce the chance of forgery.

Celebrities are advised to establish a paraph as a precaution against the rash of bootlegged autographs being sold over the internet.

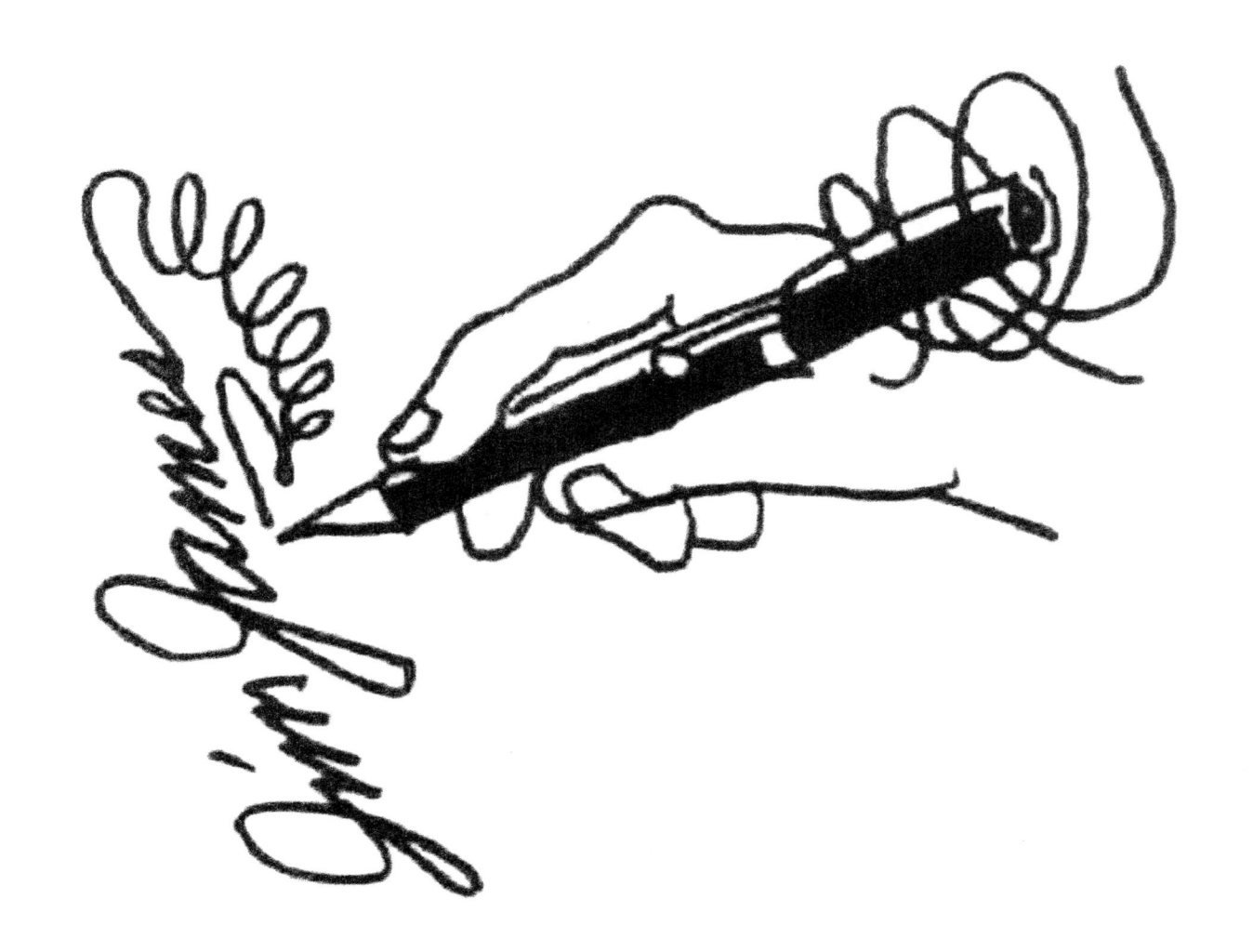

PARAPH

85) **BEDIZEN** (*bi di zan*) -- to dress in a tacky, gaudy, or tasteless way. **BEDIZENMENT** is the noun form.

It became painfully clear why certain students repeatedly dress inappropriately by some of the parental bedizenments that showed up at the PTA meeting.

BEDIZEN

86) **PANJANDRUM** (*pan jan drem*) -- a self-important or vain official or a powerful person.

We expected the ceremony to last a matter of minutes and end when the mayor cut the ribbon, but the panjandrum launched into an impromptu speech that rambled on for nearly an hour.

PANJANDRUM

87) **JEJUNE** (*ji joon*) -- lacking substance, interest, maturity, or nutritional value.

For years *A Chorus Line* held the record as the longest running show in Broadway's history, but I found the play jejune and sleazy.

JEJUNE

88) **SOLECISM** (*sol a siz em*) -- a grammatical or spoken blunder or a violation of etiquette or proper behavior.

Belinda is such a snob; she considers her brother-in-law riffraff because he committed the solecism of using the wrong fork for his salad.

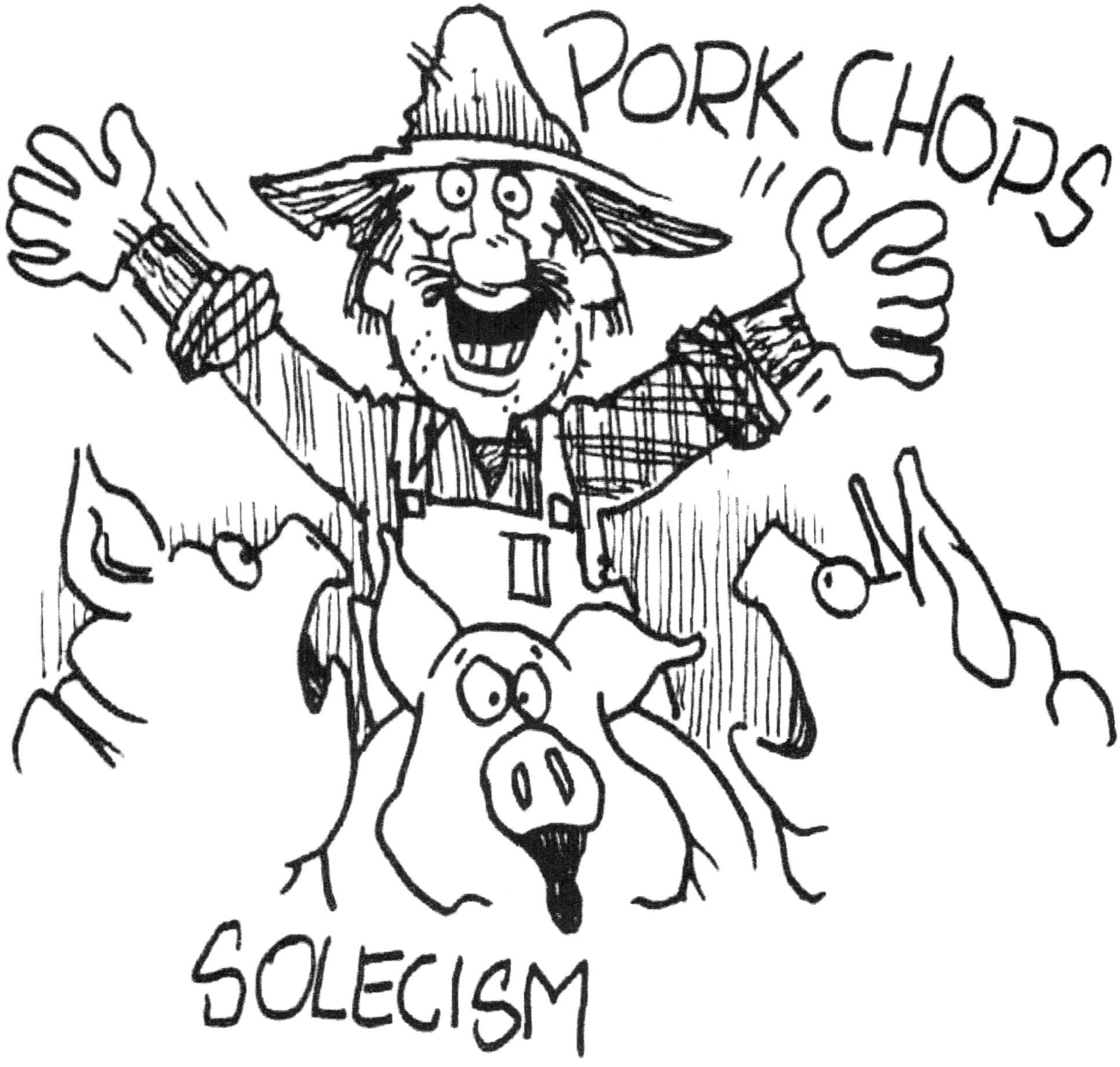
PORK CHOPS
SOLECISM

89) **BUSTEE** (*bus tee*) -- a small village or slum, generally in India, but it can be applied anywhere. It can also be spelled **BUSTI**.

Mother Teresa, who never sought fame, was as beloved in every poverty-stricken bustee as she was in the world's most affluent areas.

BUSTEE

90) **HOMUNCULUS** (*he mung kya les*) -- a small adult, a dwarf who is believed to have been created in a laboratory, or an unborn person. The plural is **HOMUNCULI**.

Snow White was very lucky to encounter seven homunculi who were so sympathetic and accommodating when she found herself in dire straits.

HOMUNCULUS

91) **CHRESTOMATHY** (*kres tom a thee*) -- a collection of written passages usually by an individual author and sometimes translated from another language.

Matthew, Mark, Luke, and John each contributed a chrestomathy to form what we now call the New Testament.

CHRESTOMATHY

92) **PSEPHOLOGY** (*see fol a jee*) -- the study of elections.

Psephologists will look back at the 2000 presidential election as a severe test of America's system of government--one that it passed with flying colors.

PSEPHOLOGY

93) **TITTLE** (*tit l*) -- a dot used in writing for punctuation or attached to a letter such as a period or the dot on a small "i" or a very small particle or quantity.

A final proofreading is essential to make sure that no words are misspelled and that none of your tittles are missing.

TITTLE

94) **NECROMANCY** (*nek ra man see*) -- magic, sorcery, or conjuring up the dead.

As incredibly popular as the Harry Potter books are, some parents are reluctant to expose their children to tales of necromancy.

NECROMANCY

95) **CICERONE** (*sis a roe nee*) --tour guide.

The cicerone who lead us through the Capitol Building was a walking congressional history book able to satisfactorily answer every single question she was asked.

CICERONE

96) **AUTEUR** (*o tur*) -- a director whose personal style, technique, or theme is evident in all his movies.

Although Orson Welles left a distinct impression in all his films, Alfred Hitchcock was certainly the most identifiable auteur of all.

AUTEUR

97) **HUSSAR** (*hoo zar*) -- a member of the 15th century Hungarian armed forces or any later European cavalry unit inspired by them, generally known for flamboyant uniforms.

The bride's maids' dresses were so ostentatious that the groom's uncle joked he was marrying into a family of hussars.

HUSSAR

98) **ELDRITCH** (*el dritch*) -- eerie, weird, foreign, or uncanny. It can also be spelled **ELDRICH** or **ELRITCH**.

There is something eldritch about that woman in the corner house; her blinds are always tightly drawn except on very overcast days when she opens them fully.

ELDRITCH

99) **VATICINATE** (*va tis a nayt*) -- predict or prophesy.

I wonder if any major event will ever occur again without some crackpot coming out of the woodwork and claiming that Nostradamus had vaticinated it.

VATICINATE

100) **ONOMATOPOEIA** (*on a mat a pee a*) -- the practice of naming something based on the sound it makes; for example "boom" or "gurgle."

Honeybees buzz about disinterestedly unaware that they have provided one of the classic example of onomatopoeia.

ONOMATOPOEIA

101) **MYRMIDON** (*mur mi don*) -- a devoted follower or servant who never questions.

To succeed as a butler one must constantly act the respectful myrmidon even if he believes that the boss is a reprehensible moron.

MYRMIDON

INDEX

Numbers in the index correspond to the words' chronological order not the page number.

A

ABSQUATULATE	30
APOTROPAIC	17
AQUILINE	81
AUTEUR	96

B

BANDERSNATCH	6
BEDIZEN	85
BILLET-DOUX	28
BILLINGSGATE	51
BRUXISM	53
BUSTEE	89

C

CAMARILLA	47
CARYATID	11
CAUDA	31
CHRESTOMATHY	91
CICERONE	95
COXCOMB	20
CREPUSCULAR	71
CRYPTOZOOLOGY	66
CYNOSURE	26

D

DADA	27
DEPILATE	54
DIPTEROUS	10
DITHYRAMBIC	56

E

ECHOLALIA	24
ECLOGUE	42
ELDRITCH	98
ELEEMOSYNARY	55
ENOLOGY	76
ENTHEOS	68
EPIPHENOMENON	32

F

FLANEUR	14
FLOCCINAUCINIHILIPILIFICATION	45
FRUGIVOROUS	33
FURPHY	4

G

GEWGAW	23
GRIFFONAGE	77
GRISAILLE	38

H

HEBDOMADAL	22
HEGIRA	57
HOMUNCULUS	90
HUSSAR	97

I

IATROGENIC	60

J

JACTITATION	34
JEFE	82
JEHU	78
JEJUNE	87

L

LEXEME	37
LIVERISH	61
LOUCHE	64
LYCANTHROPY	79

M

MINATORY	1
MISOLOGY	58
MONAD	7
MUSCIFORM	62
MYRMIDON	101

N

NECROMANCY	94
NUMINOUS	15

O

OBJICIENT	41
ONOMATOPOEIA	100
ORISON	5
OSCULATE	36

P

PANJANDRUM	86
PARADIDDLE	75
PARAPH	84
PERUKE	13
PHAETON	21
PHILODOX	52
PIED-A-TERRE	25
PLONK	46
PNEUMATOLOGY	43
PORKPIE	3
PROSCENIUM	16
PSEPHOLOGY	92
PSITTACISM	8

Q

QUANGO	50
QUIDDITY	19

R

RANTIPOLE	29
RODOMONTADE	18
RUCK	9

S

SAMIZDAT	65
SATURNALIA	74
SERAGLIO	40
SIMULACRUM	44
SOLECISM	88
SOUPCON	72
STULTILOQUENCE	67

T

TAXONOMY	80
TELAMON	12
TERGIVERSATION	59
THEOMORPHIC	49
TIFFIN	83
TINTINNABULATION	70
TITTLE	93
TRANTER	69

U

ULLAGE	2
ULULATE	39

V

VATICINATE 99
VENIRE 63

X

XIAN 35

Z

ZUGZWANG 48
ZYMOSIS 73

Hopefully you have found these 101 words educational and enjoyable. While they may not take a place in your daily conversations, many of them will come in handy on infrequent occasions. Should you have the urge to start using *bandersnatch*, *ullage*, and *floccinaucinihilipilification* on a regular basis, work diligently to stifle it!

Many of the selected *lexemes* will probably find very limited use in the average person's speaking and/or writing, but it certainly can't hurt to be familiar with any word's definition. Few of us keep an unabridged dictionary in our back pocket at all times for that rare situation when you just have to know what *paraph* means.

Knowledge is power, and having these 101 vocabulary words in your arsenal could make you deadly so use them appropriately but sparingly.

If you enjoy expanding your vocabulary, please visit the author's Word of the Day website at www.wordofthedaywebsite.com where you can subscribe for free daily emails and pick up a new word every business day.

Steven Fantina is the webmaster of Word of the Day (www.wordofthedaywebsite.com), an on-line vocabulary-building service. He is a lifelong resident of New Jersey and is available for speeches, seminars, colloquies, and any occasion where free food is provided. *101 Words You'll Probably Never Need To Know But Can Use To Impress People* is his first book. He can be reached at webmaster@wordofthedaywebsite.com.

Joel Barbee is a funny bone specialist who draws cartoons from his digs in California and invites your perusal at www.joelbarbee.com or www.portfolios.com/joelbarbee.